CHAMPIONS OF
CHANGE

Disclaimer

CONTENTS

CONTENTS

INTRODUCTION

*Never doubt that a small group of
thoughtful, committed citizens can change
the world. Indeed, it is the only thing that
ever has.*

– Margaret Mead

Are you a CEO, CIO, CFO – or other senior leader, front-line manager or project professional – who wants to ensure the success of one or many initiatives within your organisation?

This book is for you if:

- You've been trusted to lead a change program and want to get it right.

- You're excited about the work ahead, but others don't share your vision.

- Your team is fearful of new things.

- You need to execute a plan – quickly! – and don't have time or space for convoluted processes.

Five years ago, I was employed to lead change management on a large technology rollout. The business sponsor confided he wanted the rollout led by the business, not a contracted change team, to ensure success. So, I formed a champions community – a group of 'super users' and project sponsors within the business – and we didn't look back. The community members understood their colleagues' hesitancy to change their current ways of working and knew the best ways to communicate with them. In short, the community members became an important face of change. The business sponsor saw the group's potential to pivot to another related initiative, and the champions community continues to this day.

I've been deeply involved in many successful change programs just like this over the years. I've seen again and again that champions communities are absolutely key to success. However, champions are often omitted from the change process due to the time and effort required to set communities up and run them. By the end of this book, I hope to convince you that champions are not only worthwhile, but *essential* to the success of your project and organisation.

*

I've initiated and driven highly engaged and positively minded champions communities that owned, implemented and inspired change both upwards and downwards within their organisation. As well as helping to establish each community, I've enabled them to grow, develop, take ownership and run with the change themselves.

I'm fascinated by positive digital disruption and how technology can be used to make things better. I love helping people consciously create new and more inspiring futures. My aim is to *inspire* change in people rather than try to *force* them to change. I encourage groups to do something amazing and deliver transformation through human values.

I've seen change communities inspire incredible results. For example, in a recent project, 80 per cent of the organisation was happily using the new software within 12 weeks of implementation. These results came from an unscheduled audit by the champions. On another project, we received a score of four out of five in a staff survey conducted a month after a new organisational structure was implemented. (Those of you who have led or endured an organisational restructure will under-stand how rare and significant such a high score is!) The success was largely due to regular updates and support from champions to their teams.

If you want to get return on investment on perfor-mance solutions, setting up a champions community is key.

*

In this short guidebook, I will set the scene for the pace of change coming to all organisations due to the disruption of digital transformation. This will require new ways of working and collaborating.

I will talk about your organisation's capacity for change and why it is important to understand this before setting out. Organisations fail by trying to jump too many levels – for example, a government department wanting to become like Uber within a single step, or a private entity trying to implement a project that is far from fitting its current culture.

I will cover the four key components of an extended change community and where the champions fit, then dig into a three-phase approach to set up a champions network and build the approach, then launch and sustain the community.

I'll outline why creating this community is so important for success, and what you can do to create your own highly engaged champions of change.

Read on to discover:

- How digital transformation is changing everything

- How to assess your organisation's capacity for change and tailor your approach based on that

- The benefits of champions

- How to use the three-phase approach to set up a champions network:

    1. Build the approach and framework

    2. Launch it by kicking off your recruitment process, then the community

    3. Sustain, nurture and support the community to ensure it stays relevant and vibrant.

[illegible] who [illegible] community [illegible] for [illegible] with highly engaged [illegible] [illegible] discover [illegible]

[illegible] everything

How to assess [illegible] organisation's capacity [illegible] and tailor [illegible] based on that

The benefits of champions

How to use the [illegible] phase approach to set up a champions network

1. Build the approach and framework

2. Launch by kicking off your recruitment process, then the community

3. Sustain, nurture and support the community to ensure it stays relevant and vibrant.

1

THE DIGITAL IMPERATIVE – SETTING THE CONTEXT

Digital transformation impacts entire industries and businesses. Digital transformation means integrating digital technology into how you operate to deliver value to customers and employees. To do this you need to change your organisational culture. It means being agile – nimble and quick to adapt.

An agile company embraces innovation, challenges the status quo, experiments and gets comfortable with testing, failing fast and iterating – it is built into its DNA. The most agile companies are the best positioned to survive the inevitable move to a digital business model.

Transformation is not a single change or event. It is not incremental. It is a set of major changes for customers and employees and the impact is wide and deep. Transformations happen across multiple years through business cycles and transition states as artificial intelligence (AI) and digital technology shape our world. Agile organisations can stay resilient and adapt to constant change. Organisations that can adapt to changing workplace dynamics will thrive, not just survive.

Digital transformation is not about one or two technology projects aligned to your strategy. It's about disrupting your business's bottom line and adapting to constant and complex change. The change will be across people and process, redefining target operating models. Often it also means maintaining the old model of doing business alongside the new – for example, banks offer digital business and operating models while maintaining branches and call centres.

In this chapter I'll share examples of what's going on across the business world. The evidence is clear: you need to act. It's essential to understand the context because if you don't, you may feel that you have more time than you think. But there's no time to think. You need to work on strategies now to catch up with and surpass your competitors. This book gives you a key ingredient that will help you build a collaborative culture.

Most digital transformation programs fail – not due to lack of ambition or strategy, but poor execution. Digital transformation does not respect traditional organisational boundaries. Instead, you need to change corporate culture and break down silos. Collaboration, a key ingredient, is essential but not always easy.

It is vital to align with your organisation's strategic goals and objectives. Understanding your current organisational maturity and ways of working is key. Building autonomy, risk-taking and the right leadership is critical and underpinned by the right organisational roles and structure – and champions of change.

HERE'S WHY

A 2017 study by PricewaterhouseCoopers (PwC) calculated the global GDP would be 14 per cent higher by 2030 due to AI adoption, contributing an additional US$15.7 trillion to the global economy. The creation of enormous data oceans allows AI to predict your next move. Everything around you is now connected – or soon will be. It's the Internet of Things. Trains, planes, cars, washing machines, wind turbines, buildings, ovens, buoys out in the ocean, clothes and even shoes can be set up to feed into this sea of data, revealing how they get used or could be used better. This data is logged, analysed and interpreted by machines.

In a recent study, Gartner, a global research and advisory firm providing information, advice, and tools for leaders, predicted that by 2024, 69 per cent of routine work currently done by managers will be fully automated. Organisations will be working with robotic process automation (RPA). RPA is the fastest-growing enterprise software category. Emerging technologies such as AI, machine learning and blockchain are game changers. They are the drivers of digital transformation within existing industries and are also shaping new jobs and industries.

AI in manufacturing is part of a more significant trend towards automated production. With the development of intelligent factories, AI systems can transform the way companies run their production lines. It enables greater efficiency by enhancing human capabilities, providing real-time insights and facilitating design and product innovation.

Here's a summary demonstrating the breadth of innovations across many industries:

- Manufacturers can predict toxins in grains of food.

- Smart factories have transformed the way production lines are run.

- Transport companies can predict arrival times or issues.

- Scientists can learn how to treat cancer more effectively.

- Farmers can grow more food using fewer natural resources.

- Health departments can view single digital health records and patient portals.

- Restaurants can connect their cloud-based application with their payment gateway and logistics teams.

- Hospitals can use the Tissue Analytics app to help analyse, treat and monitor chronic wounds and integrate this with the electronic medical record system so images and data can be stored, reviewed and compared.

- Data analytic platforms can build, embed and deploy analytic apps to drive engagement, empower users and surface deeper insights easily.

- Digital currencies have decentralised banking and will do away with the need for a central bank. These currencies can be sent from user to user on peer-to-peer networks.

- Blockchain is a system of recording information in a way that makes it difficult or impossible to change, hack or cheat the system. A blockchain is a ledger of digital transactions that is duplicated and distributed across the entire network of computer systems on the blockchain.

This gives an insight into the breadth of these changes. Let's now look at more specific case studies.

The Centre for Computational Science in Western Japan has a computer almost three times more powerful than any other computer the world has ever seen. It combines the power of 160,000 processing units and performs tasks that would have taken its predecessors an entire year in a few days. It deals with the problem of the spread of invisible coronavirus droplets by making the virus visible. By using simulations, it has figured out that the ideal height for office partitions is 1.4 metres. If the partition is too high – for example, 1.6 metres – it reduces the ventilation capacity in the room and creates a situation where aerosols can stick around for a long time.

Apart from the supercomputer simulating the virus, it also searches for drugs that can fight the symptoms in a database of more than 2000 potential treatments and has already found some promising results. The computer compares the existing medications with everything we know about COVID-19, looking for any matches by simulating how it could bind to proteins unique to the virus and how the drug will work in the body. It predicts how the invisible virus can spread in a crucial step to contain it and help society move one step closer to normality.

In fintech, superfunds have been pouring money into AI and improving mobile apps to harness an uptick in member engagement using AI and mobile data.

The manufacturing industry invests in technology to take advantage of automation, robotics, AI, optimised technologies and data-driven systems. The industry is funding research to use these technologies to:

- build smart factories

- enable predictive machine and infrastructure maintenance

- improve data security in large sensor networks

- optimise supply chains using new logistic models

- predict toxins in food grains.

I'm telling you this to demonstrate the impact technology is having on all industries right now. Change is escalating at a fast pace. Want some more examples?

UNSW researchers, in partnership with Onesteel, developed a green steel product using recycled rubber tyres, which prevented over two million car tyres from going to landfill.

Sydney Local Health District is trialling an app that uses AI to help analyse, treat and monitor chronic wounds. Royal Prince Alfred Hospital in Sydney is trialling the Tissue Analytics app, which integrates with the hospital's Cerner electronic medical record so images and data can be stored, reviewed and compared.

The Australian banking industry is on the cusp of a second revolution in the contactless payments market, which promises to deliver cheaper service plans to small businesses. Local banks are reconfiguring their merchant service offerings to accommodate a new mobile payments technology that will slash the cost of point-of-sale transactions and expand the number of small businesses connected to the interchange system.

There are sensors already around us in our workplaces, cars, homes and cities. Rapid advancements in technologies are changing the way humans interact with their environment. The Internet of Things connects everyday objects to the internet, sharing and sending data to make daily life easier and make cities safe, livable and dynamic.

A range of utilities, including Sydney Water, are looking at emerging technologies to help predict and prevent critical failures in water supply infrastructure.

In space and aviation, autonomous aircraft and robotics-powered positioning, navigation and timing are all developments coming out of the rapid growth of the Australian civil space industry.

In the environment and agtech sectors, new technologies have enabled real-time and efficient air and water quality monitoring. AI has also improved harvesting and yield efficiency and food chain quality assurance by measuring soil nutrient content, moisture, potassium, nitrogen and phosphorus levels to provide farmers with smart metrics for making decisions. Livestock monitoring uses thermal and motion sensors to measure the health of cattle. Agtech specialists are analysing soil density and determining the amount of water needed.

Australia is a leading contributor to medtech innovation. Sensors have been developed to monitor health and wellbeing markers, such as fine and coarse movements. These can also monitor vital signs such as heart rate, respiration rate, blood pressure, temperature and musculoskeletal motion. Sun exposure sensors can alert people to sun overexposure.

The resources and energy sector is developing and deploying innovation to increase extraction, improve processes and minimise the risk of damage to the environment and employees.

You may think your industry is exempt from this type of change, despite this overwhelming evidence. But this chapter highlights a minuscule slice of the data and revolutions taking place across all industries. If you still think you're exempt, consider the case of the big banks of the banking industry – a safe, regulated industry dominated by the Big Four, who believed they were untouchable. Then blockchain technology came along, along with Bitcoin and other cryptocurrencies offering an alternative to the standard monetary system. Other fintech solutions are being developed and brought to market every day.

LEADERSHIP IS KEY

Leaders help themselves and others to do the right things. For any big change project, leaders need to build an inspiring vision, set direction and create something new. But you do not need to do it all alone. Being a great leader means trusting others to help you bring home the change. Sometimes that is hard. Leadership in this context is building the right ecosystem, mapping out where you need to go as a team or an organisation and handing over the reins to a thriving change community to help you bring it home. Change champions are a key component to building an informal leadership ecosystem.

Over time you can build a culture that values courage to lead, and that encourages people to step out of their comfort zones. That also means stepping out of your leadership comfort zone without feeling threatened or insecure.

People often experience real vulnerability when going through change. Leaders are no different. Building a support network can help you success-fully manage and lead through change.

CONCLUSION

Today's business environment is too dynamic to manage change on a project basis. Organisations must stay agile and resilient to adapt to constant change, as AI and digital technologies shape our world. Those who can adapt to changing work-place dynamics will not only survive but thrive. Personalised and rich digital experience on any device is what new and old companies that have pivoted are delivering. The shift is to offering online digital services and is a threat to many industries.

Stop thinking that this won't happen to you or that technological change is a tech issue. It is a leader-ship issue.

Create a burning platform, get clear on the tech-nology changes in your industry and how you can benefit from them, and get your organisation focus-ing on this long-term thinking and your roadmap while managing business as usual.

In the next chapter, we will look at the importance of benchmarking your organisation's capacity for change, why it is essential, some tools and frameworks to consider and the agile approach to take to this solution.

Take action

- Research the emerging technologies related to your industry. Read industry news and business media. Check out what your competitors are doing. Follow them on social media.

- Put change on the agenda. Ask your team to bring one idea for innovation or improvement to every team meeting.

- Raise change with your manager. Share what you've learned. Discuss the risks of *not* keeping pace with the industry. Become a champion for change.

2

THE CAPACITY TO CHANGE

Before your organisation can change, you need to get a clear view of its current capability. Traditional approaches to managing volatility, uncertainty, complexity and ambiguity focus on formal risk and compliance. The aim is to control internal compliance and contingency planning. Traditional approaches come with a high cost: less flexibility and responsiveness, for limited gains.

Emerging approaches focus on organisational maturity and capabilities. It takes a systemic approach, which enhances the organisation's ability to anticipate and respond to trends and opportunities for change and transformation. This enables the system to become more productive and collaborative. This new approach is what I will cover in this chapter.

There are ever-increasing levels of volatility and ambiguity for most industries. Organisations need to get 'change fit'. They can be too ambitious and fail by trying to jump too many levels in one go.

In this chapter, I will provide some examples of companies that have attempted a big leap and failed. We're going to look at the new research into assessing capability as a success factor in digital business transformations.

THE MISSING SUCCESS FACTOR

Organisations often overlook one crucial thing: their organisational capacity to change. This leads to a low return on investment and lack of success. There are many examples of change failures, lots of money spent and benefits not realised.

It is crucial not to start by tinkering around the edges or working on separate siloed projects. Instead, the focus should be on enhancing the organisation's capacity to change, which means shifting organisational culture and building agility. I'm not talking about managing change project by project – I'm talking about managing change systematically across the enterprise and building change leadership capability.

It will save money and time. It will enable you to tailor the approach, providing the right amount of change in line with existing cultural practices. If you assess your current culture this will inform the pace of change your organisation can cope with for digital transformation to work and strengthen the organisation.

A leadership ecosystem is required to lead a successful transformation across the entire organisation. The right management to support that vision for change is crucial. A thriving champions community is part of the ecosystem.

Most organisational change efforts take longer and cost more money than leaders and managers anticipate. If you are in a super-conservative organisation like a bank, making the leap to an Amazon or Uber-style business is too big. You need to go from one development stage to the next. It is very hard jumping too many levels.

STAGES OF ORGANISATIONAL MATURITY

The lowest stage of organisational maturity is when a company is risk averse; is disorganised, with absent leadership; and has a culture that doesn't reward collaboration. At the highest level of organisational maturity, successful leaders encourage experimentation; they have baked collaboration into tools and systems. With a focus on building the right culture it is easier to manage change.

Like change management, there are many models and methodologies to measure and track organisational capability and maturity. For example, the Organisation Capability Maturity Framework devised by the Organisation Development Tools Institute documents seven levels of organisation capability. The IDC Future IT Maturity Assessment has a five-stage model of organisational maturity. See the 'take action' breakout at the end of this chapter for links to these models.

You might be thinking:

- that you have delivered many successful change projects over the years

- that digital change won't impact your industry

- that you already have a good understanding of the culture in your organisation right now

- that your organisation has a successful strategy in place for the next five years.

Think again. Benchmarking your organisation against proven frameworks and bodies of knowledge will test your current thinking and either validate it or challenge it to make adjustments.

Agile companies such as Netflix and Google understand this, and have built high-performing cultures that embrace collaboration and agility from the very start. Even these companies need to ensure the right culture and practices remain in place to foster collaboration and change.

A ROADMAP FOR CHANGE

Often a critical roadblock to bringing a change vision to life is asking too much of employees without the right processes, practices, leadership and culture in place for the leap required.

Common barriers include:

- organisational inertia

- the rate of change in flight

- poor leadership

- a weak culture not aligned with the mission

- lack of participation and buy-in

- under-communicating a strong vision

- overcommunicating a poor vision

- not enough training or resources

- change fatigue

- past values playing on the minds of employees and the sacrifices made during an arduous change process.

It is wise to benchmark your current state, envision your future state and identify the gaps in a roadmap to get there to ensure the right pace and approach.

CONCLUSION

If a transformation is not pitched to the right cap-ability, or it's poorly led, fatigue can set in because you're asking too much of employees. Remember, we're going to start small and build the organisation you want incrementally – starting with where you are now.

In the next chapter we'll dig into the importance of change champions and how to form a community of champions.

Take action

- Work with leaders in your organisation as well as your wider team to benchmark your current state – your capacity for change.

- Use an organisational capability tool to benchmark your organisation, give you a starting point and inform the rate of change that will suit your organisation. Suggested tools include:

  - orgcmf.com/en-gb/pages/home

  - idc.com/itexecutive/planning-guides/maturity-assessment

- Create a vision of your desired future state.

- Identify the gaps between your future vision and your current state.

- Take action to address those gaps.

3

CHAMPIONS AND YOUR CHANGE COMMUNITY

In this chapter, I will talk about champions. What is a champion and why should you use them? To put champions into context, I'll also cover the roles and responsibilities within the extended change community.

Champions are internal employees who like learning new technology and helping their colleagues. They are an important but often neglected part of the extended change ecosystem. Champions aren't leaders, managers or support teams – they're the employees at the coalface. A champions community is a collaborative, informal network of people who will be there long after the project has been implemented.

You need to form an extended change community and spend the time growing, building and supporting this group. This means your change will be successful from the get-go right through to transitioning to business as usual where the project is no longer in the development or implementation phase. Champions are a key part of this extended change community. They are the go-to workplace support people who answer user questions and help drive engagement.

Learning via coworkers is among the most effective and most-used methods for supporting the workforce. This has been proven via several studies, including as recently as 2021 when a team from Princeton University found that learning from coworkers is significant.

Let's delve into the four key components of an extended change community and what change champions are.

THE FOUR KEY COMPONENTS OF A CHANGE COMMUNITY

Change is always best if it's business-led rather than project-led. This means building a change community consisting of four key subgroups:

1. Business sponsors, business owners, product owners and subject matter experts (SMEs).

2. Managers, leaders, and support functions such as the IT service desk, for example.

3. Champions of change.

4. Project delivery team, including change communications and learning specialists.

Setting up a change community is about engaging the leaders and operations, and building your change community. This book focuses on building your change champions network, an often neglected ingredient. There has been plenty written about managers and leaders, but not enough about change champions.

It is important to define the key roles and responsibilities in managing change. This makes the roles and responsibilities clear for the people identified. Let's take a look at them now.

Business sponsors, business owners, product owners and SMEs

This group participates actively and visibly throughout the delivery. They communicate their support and promote the change and benefits. They are proactive and use their networks and influence to manage obstacles and resistance to change. They can keep their peers up-to-date about the components that may impact or interest them and talk through their concerns. It's a big part of their role to recognise and reward people whose behaviours support a successful transition and ongoing embedding of the change. They can also support frontline managers as they move along the change curve, ensuring that commitment to change is achieved and sustained.

Managers, leaders and support functions
Those in this group can lead their teams through the change transition and embedding period. They can support individuals to understand the change and why the company is changing. They take responsibility for:

- overseeing change readiness activities and plans

- updating relevant performance metrics

- contributing to communications and engagement plans

- ensuring commitment, reinforcing messages and listening to and acting on feedback

- providing feedback to the project delivery team about what is working or not working

- identifying and managing resistance to change with the support of the change specialists in the project delivery team as necessary

- recognising and rewarding team members who demonstrate the right behaviours, supporting change success

- sharing these success stories

- supporting the change champions in overcoming roadblocks.

Champions of change

The third group is the change champions, who can prepare their colleagues and team to understand the change, and be ready and supportive. They can provide input into impact assessments, change, training approaches and plans. They can:

- share communications

- create momentum and engagement before going live and during the launch

- raise issues and concerns, and gather feedback from teams on the ground to share with the project delivery team

- support the project delivery team with the communications and training activities

- support their team as SMEs in the lead-up, rollout and transition to business as usual.

Project delivery team

The fourth group comprises the change, communications and learning specialists assigned to the project. Their role is to plan and deliver change and oversee the ongoing embedding activities to build awareness and support for the change, in partnership with business leaders, managers and SMEs. They can understand, highlight and manage the change impacts and risks to ensure that the business stakeholders make a smooth transition. They can enable end users to build knowledge and skills in the new processes and systems through an effective learning approach. They support business leaders, team managers, champions and SMEs to manage issues, field questions and gather feedback. They can also provide coaching advice to the business leaders, SMEs and change champions in leading and embedding the change in their teams.

Some of the most successful change projects I've seen have been effective due to the large, thriving champions network supported by project and business leaders and then continued once the project was rolled out. For example, on a technology rollout across a large, siloed organisation, the champions community became our path to the business. My program manager always backed me, but others on the project didn't. It took six months to get traction with the group. It became an important forum to consult and for the project to showcase solutions.

WHAT ROLES DO CHAMPIONS PLAY IN THE CHANGE COMMUNITY?

A change champion is a person at any level of the organisation who's skilled at initiating, facilitating and implementing change. Change champions support and promote change from within their teams and regions. They are the driving force of organisational change – leading their colleagues and teams towards innovation. They can be closely linked to the initiative owners across the business and supported by the head of change.

Champions are people who can evangelise and help train their teams on a new system or in new ways of working. They build awareness, understanding and engagement for their team. In the end, they become the key to the success of the project both during and after delivery. Champions will help drive engagement throughout the organisation and reduce the strain on the resources of the core project delivery team.

You can have specific types of champions. You can have project-specific champions for the project you're promoting if it is a big system. You can also have collaboration champions, business process improvement champions, knowledge management champions and digital transformation champions. It's about defining the scope of this group and equipping them to deliver what your business needs.

For example, at a large health organisation I worked at, we had a lively group of champions including frontline hospital staff, mental health workers, aged care workers, managers and people from head office who were championing new ways of working and how to get the most out of the collaboration technology within their context. They ran weekly mental health support groups to do ward rounds during COVID-19.

It is important to define the champions' role and purpose. For example, when I rolled out collaboration technology for a large financial services company, we appointed collaboration champions to get to know the technology and promote new ways of working and being productive online. In another project, we tapped into the existing champions network to promote our collaboration technology as there was a substantial document knowledge management component in this project for knowledge management. They were an established group and respected throughout the business, and they were a great network to leverage for other things. (But be careful not to overload them.)

In 2020, Microsoft studied the effectiveness of using learning methods versus getting help from others. They found that utilising coworkers who were not part of the project team or IT service desks was the most effective.

THE CONSEQUENCES OF NOT HAVING CHANGE CHAMPIONS

Change is often met with resistance. You can improve your odds of success if the voices championing change belong to workers and not just upper management. Recruiting frontline employees to share the need for change (and the benefits) with their peers can speed up awareness and buy-in, decrease resistance, help gather feedback and disseminate information about planned change initiatives. If you don't have change champions to do this, the project team will have to guess what people are saying, doing and feeling.

Changes often fail when a gap emerges between sponsor announcements and subsequent local actions. Research has repeatedly shown that employees pay most attention to messages received from their immediate boss and team. Without strong, local sponsorship and a thriving change community there is less likelihood of employees adopting the change. Strong resistance could quickly emerge and not be addressed.

The role of local change champions is to connect the work done at the organisational level to the change at the local level. If you don't have champions it's likely your project will comprise installation at best, rather than implementation.

Remember, champions need to have their concerns and needs about the change addressed before they can articulate the benefits of change to their team.

CONCLUSION

In this chapter, you have learned about the importance of building a thriving change ecosystem and the four key ingredients of it. This sets you up to become an agile, innovative organisation. We then focused on the importance of change champions and forming a community of champions. You need to start thinking about the project and who could be your champions of change. Leverage existing communities and pivot them to your project or think about setting up a new community from scratch. Getting the champions program up and running in your organisation is beneficial to any project they are part of, but it will also benefit your organisation as a whole when you start thinking about those long-range goals you want to achieve.

In the next chapter, we will discuss the key benefits of change champions, what they do, the impact they have and some of the challenges they face.

Take action

· Start identifying the roles and responsibilities your change ecosystem requires.

· Write down how you would use your champions in your current change project.

· Think about some likely champion candidates within your team or organisation.

4

THE BENEFITS AND CHALLENGES OF ESTABLISHING A CHAMPIONS COMMUNITY

This chapter is about why you should use change champions, what they do, their business benefits, the impact they can have and some of the challenges of being a champion. It is important to be strategic when forming a champions community. Always think through the benefits, impacts and potential challenges before starting to recruit.

Champions have a positive influence on the values and beliefs of a culture, which reduces resistance to change. There is value in forming a group of internal staff at the local level to become a network of adoption specialists. Staff trust their peers to advise and direct them.

Champions bring local knowledge of how things work in the organisation, married with an in-depth knowledge of new tools and software capabilities, to bring change to life for their team or division.

Many people are afraid or hesitant to step into their leadership capacity and need support and encouragement to get there. Your champions forum is a great place to coach and mentor this group. We will discuss champions forums later in this book.

A champions program allows organisations to leverage individuals from within. Studies have shown that users are engaged when their concerns and questions are addressed at a local level, and they feel they are part of something bigger than themselves.

A champions program is beneficial for your project and your organisation as a whole. Champions help you achieve long-range organisational goals. The key is to align the group to the organisation's strategic vision or your program vision.

Change champions are particularly successful in the early adoption of the change process, motivating others to try alternative work practices and systems. The social influence of the champion is fundamental. A champion sets a tone and mood for response to change, provides information and peer support, and can also offer formal or informal coaching to increase staff understanding of the benefits of change. By working alongside their colleagues who are affected by change implementation, the champion can use multiple modes of delivery to aid learning and understanding, and make sense of the change. But they need to be trained and supported.

Senior leadership must confidently lead a digital workforce, drive a culture of transformation and help the champions foster the growth mindset required for their long-term success.

WHY USE CHANGE CHAMPIONS?

Organisations don't change, people do. One of the most effective methods for influencing change is through peer-to-peer support. Establishing a well-supported change champion network is an extraordinarily successful approach to implementing sustained change within an organisation. As I mentioned earlier in the book, learning from coworkers is among the most effective and most-used methods.

Similar concepts to that of change champion have been successfully used for decades to embed specific behaviours within organisations – for example, health and safety, environment or compliance officers.

Champions support and help by reducing the strain on the resources of the core project team and driving engagement throughout the organisation. Champions will help scale by advocating for the change and helping train their teams on the new ways of working. They build awareness, understanding and engagement throughout the organisation.

The 2020 Microsoft survey I mentioned in chapter 3 found that champions perform their role because it makes their job easier when others around them know how to use the solution. They like to be recognised for their expertise and efforts, and respond well to a formalised program of training and regular forums. They're adding to their professional development, but certification doesn't seem to be a prime motivator.

At UNSW, we appointed a tier of senior leaders within the champions group and defined KPIs. We also worked with HR to get members of the champions leadership group an annual bonus for doing that role. They became instrumental in guiding new functionality and builds – prioritising what needed to be built, letting the business know and helping the IT service desk, as well as being an ongoing part of the whole governance of the platform.

Building an internal group of business adoption champions is your sweet spot. They have the local knowledge of how the business works. For example, at a recent healthcare client, I recruited 70 champions across private, public, healthcare and aged care divisions. Each of them contributed their divisional expertise and communicated the nuances of issues their people were facing.

THE BUSINESS BENEFITS OF A CHANGE CHAMPIONS COMMUNITY

Some of the business benefits of forming a champions community include:

- Reduced pressure on the centralised team to deliver change

- Ability to identify issues on the ground and raise them quickly to the project delivery team

- Ability to gather feedback on the communications campaign and communicate this to the project delivery team

- Increased capacity to identify and manage the resistors of change at a local level

- Increased capacity within teams – champions become super users and therefore assist with user training in new systems, but also in new ways of working

- A forum for them to support each other, brainstorm ideas and showcase ideas to their peers.

There is nothing more important for change than having people at the coalface with a deep local knowledge, a thorough understanding of what the project is delivering and the ability to connect the two to their teams.

One of the champions within my healthcare client's team was keen to deliver a mental health support group to 20 participants using the new collaboration technology we were implementing, while addressing privacy issues. We worked through that and, in doing so, she understood the challenges and articulated them well. She ran a pilot and it became an instrumental piece of technology for the team – being able to continue as usual and connect with this mental health support group during the pandemic.

The champions will be participating actively in the group that you form and sharing knowledge, but they will also be challenging some of the ideas and advocating for their users. It comes down to how lively the community is and how they trust they're being supported. You need to be able to support them as well as the project. It takes time and effort to build these communities, but it pays off in the long run.

BENEFITS FOR CHAMPIONS

Your change champions need to be nurtured. You must have a clear understanding of what you're asking them to do, and what support and training they may require to step into their new leadership role.

A change champion has a strong sense of involvement. Membership of a champions community promotes ownership of the change and a desire to succeed. Champions communities encourage individual confidence, job satisfaction and a sense of belonging within a group.

Champions are often extremely proud of their membership of the group. I've heard champions say things like:

- 'I am a power user. It's about sharing ideas. I will share my knowledge and encourage others to keep going.'

- 'Part of my job is to encourage community and knowledge sharing. I need to find the people who are motivated. I see this role as an opportunity.'

One participant in a large program used the experience she gained as champion to transition to her leadership role. We gave her training in presentation skills. She was quite nervous at first, but in the end she took over running the forums and would present challenges she was facing within her team back to the forum, and then they would brainstorm how to solve it. People gained a much clearer insight into some of the things that she was advocating to build, as well as how she was supporting her team. She was a great role model within that network and it was just a matter of nurturing her latent skills and talents, and giving her an opportunity.

THE CHALLENGES A CHANGE CHAMPION FACES

The list below gives the main barriers change champions, as well as change managers and business leaders, face when making change:

- underestimating the complexity of systemic change

- time constraints in regular work days

- competing priorities

- engaging and maintaining participation in their team

- volume or complexity of data collection

- work schedules, assignments and other responsibilities

- inconsistent messaging

- lack of clarity and unclear expectations of champions from the project and the business

- lack of leadership support

- lack of management support for the change

- system-wide and organisational barriers

- lack of research to support implementation of champion roles and expectations

- lack of first-level leadership support to facilitate change by the champion

- lack of ongoing training and development.

These are things that can impact the success of your champions community, and you need to be monitoring them. It comes down to how successfully you're communicating your change and supporting your leaders, while also simplifying and telling the business why you're doing this. A common problem is not articulating the role, time commitment and KPIs back to the manager to give their staff member time to perform the champions role.

It's important to be purposeful about forming your change community and set it up for success by taking a coordinated approach to establishing and maintaining the network. This ensures that these challenges are either removed or minimised, and provides a forum for the champions to be able to voice their concerns – as long as you're building their trust.

I had some doctors in a healthcare champions group who were obviously very busy in the workplace. They wanted to be involved but often couldn't get to meetings. You have to find a way of being able to manage that.

Until the group gains its own momentum and you've formed a trusted network of people and a knowledge-sharing network, you need someone dedicated to form this community and build momentum. It's like any group of humans: it takes time for barriers to come down, trust to be built and it to become a safe forum where they can get support, air their issues and their successes, and be rewarded for it.

CONCLUSION

You have learned about the benefits of having a change champion network, the impacts on them and some of the challenges they may face as a group. You will also face these challenges and need to address them as the group coordinator.

Start rallying these individuals in your organisation and get them engaged, so they can assist you as they become ambassadors for the change alongside you.

In the next chapter, we will be looking at how to attract, build and get support for the community.

Take action

- Think about the benefits of forming a champions community for you, the project and the organisation.

- Start listing potential candidates. Include their name, employee ID, manager and contact details. This will become a key artefact for you to be able to communicate to their managers and then to the group.

- Consider the challenges your community members may face that are unique to your organisation.

5

PHASE 1 – DEVELOP THE APPROACH AND FRAMEWORK

As you now know, your champions community is one of the key components of your wider change ecosystem. Now it's time to start building the group and prepare them to support and promote change from within their teams, regions or countries – depending on the size and reach of the organisation. If you do this right, champions will become a driving force of organisational change, leading their colleagues and teams towards your new systems, processes, ways of working and innovation. They will support leaders and teams with their on-the-ground knowledge.

Plan well to form this community but bear in mind, it's a marathon not a sprint. Get prepared to devote time and effort to nurture and build this thriving community that will become your key organisational asset.

As I mentioned in the introduction, we'll use a three-phase approach to set up a champions network. First, build the approach and framework – finalise the structure, build a plan and engage people managers. Second, launch it – kick off the recruitment process, then the community and set up an online place to collaborate. Third, sustain it by nurturing, building and supporting the community to stay relevant and vibrant. Much energy and thought needs to be put into all three phases. It is vital to assign a person to manage this process, and build and support the community. It can save time and money to hire a specialist to manage these tasks as it can be time consuming, and an outside perspective is always useful.

This chapter delves into phase 1: developing the approach and framework.

DOCUMENTING YOUR PROJECT

Now it's time to plan and document your approach. Champions need a clear scope and view of the benefits of joining the champions community. When that is clear, it is easier to send consistent positive reinforcement to affirm their efforts. To do this successfully, treat it as a project – build a clear plan and execute against it, then manage it like any other project. This means developing a charter for the community and clearly setting out the scope, commitment and expectations. Get it signed off by your key stakeholders in the project.

The first step is to appoint a project manager who will manage the community and initial recruitment. Often the change lead can fulfil this role during the life of the project, but it's vital to earmark an employee who will be there long after the project has been deployed. This is the difference between success and failure.

WRITING YOUR CHARTER

A clear charter is a great artefact to market the benefits of the champions community to people you need to support it, as well as when recruiting participants. Your charter will help you get clear on where the champions fit and identify any existing champion networks you could leverage.

When it's time to write your charter, start by answering the following questions:

· Which initiative will the champions be attached to?

- Where does this community sit in the engagement activities?

- Where does it sit in terms of other champion networks already established in the organisation?

- What is the purpose of the community?

- What are their accountabilities?

- What is the process for recruiting and meeting regularly?

- Who are the primary attendees?

- Who are the secondary attendees and interested parties?

- Who is your executive sponsor? (You need a respected executive sponsor to help promote and advocate for the community in senior leadership channels and to all staff.)

- Who are your key stakeholders to sign this off?

Then, draft a charter that includes:

- Purpose – what is the change your champions are advocating for and supporting?

- Attendees – who is attending and why?

- Governance – what is the governance structure that will underpin your project? How will your champions give feedback to see ongoing improvements and progress?

- Cadence – how often will you will meet? (For example, fortnightly or monthly.)

- Standing agenda items – these could include project updates and champion updates.

- How you plan to run it – will it be formal or informal? Will there be guest speakers, champions running mini training sessions, or opportunities for champions to ask the group for advice and guidance on how to solve problems and issues?

CHAMPIONS ROLE DESCRIPTION

It helps to write a clear role description to share with managers first and then the champions. This may mean developing a cutdown version for the champions. The role of the change champion should be an official part of the individual's broader role, written into their job description and forming part of performance and development planning.

Writing a role description will help you get clear on the type of person you're looking for and assess whether people have the skills or potential to perform this role. This is an important artefact to share with supporters, potential candidates and new starters. It will give each champion a clear scope and they will then know what to expect.

Here is an example of a champions role description.

Champions role description

As a champion you:

- like learning new technology and helping your colleagues

- know how to get the most out of new technology tools

- know which application to use, when and how

- are the go-to person in your team when it comes to tech issues

- understand the importance of sharing knowledge

- are across benefits, updates and new releases.

Your role is to:

- communicate, problem-solve, influence, show and tell

- create the groundswell and enthusiasm to encourage adoption of improved ways of working

- build a circle of influence among your teams

- bring new ways of working to life across your teams

- identify business challenges and possible solutions

- provide feedback to the project team and sponsors

- build awareness of the technology, process and/or organisational change through informal communication channels.

As the local subject matter expert you will have access to product training, additional tools and other early adopter opportunities.

BUILDING AN INITIAL CANDIDATE LIST

It's time to come up with an initial list of people you would like to launch with in your first meeting.

A change champion can be an influencer at any level of the organisation – already skilled in initiating, facilitating and implementing the change – or someone who has the potential to step into a change leadership role. You will often find your champions where you least expect to. For example, in one project I was involved with, a contact centre employee who became influential within the community and also to management. She wasn't high on the organisational hierarchy, but had natural leadership abilities and was a great communicator – a skill she further developed in her champion role. She saw an opportunity and went for it.

You should also list the potential candidates' managers and the initiative owners you're aligning to. You need to have discussions with department leaders and managers across different lines of business to help locate thought leaders, technology evangelists and other people that you think would be suitable for this role. Thought leaders and technology evangelists tend to make good champions of change.

You need to develop your overall coverage plan – for example, the number of champions per office, department, team, floor and so on. This enables you to get the right representation across the organisation.

On one project, I made the mistake of not building a list with all the relevant information about each individual at the outset. This meant that I had to take two days out to track all my emails and instant messages, build the list and manually search who each of their managers were. Having learned my lesson, in the next project I got a list of all employees from the HR system and used this data to build my champions list. This was much quicker and more accurate, as the HR system data was up-to-date.

Use a spreadsheet to capture the following details:

- country, if relevant

- division

- team

- name

- email

- phone number

- their role in the business

- manager's name

- manager's role

- manager's email

- champion start date.

You can then filter your spreadsheet by division, team or manager, and use it as your master distribution list.

TALKING TO THE PEOPLE MANAGERS

You need to articulate the value of the champions community to the organisation to get support from key stakeholders. The earlier you can start this, the better. The first step is to contact managers via email or meeting, to either nominate or ask for volunteer change champions.

You can engage the people managers either one-on-one or as a group meeting. Be clear about the role and its benefits first. Be clear on what you want and why – make sure you have already written your charter and role description, so you are well prepared. You should include the following in your communication:

- discuss the role description

- discuss the level of involvement and time commitment required

- outline the value the champions community will bring to the manager and the team

- share the group's charter

- ask for nominations of potential candidates

- get commitment from the manager to support the time required for champions contribution

- invite the managers to the champions kickoff meeting as optional attendees.

It's a good idea to provide the manager with an email template to send to the nominees, or a template requesting volunteers.

Partnering with certain people managers who are enthusiastic about the project can be a great way to get other managers on board. For example, in a recent project I partnered with a senior manager to present to an existing information management champion network across 14 departments. This was to:

- create awareness of the new technology being rolled out

- create understanding of managing information on the new platform

- get them interested in volunteering for the new collaboration champion role

- encourage their team members to volunteer.

FINALISING YOUR COMMUNITY DESIGN

Work with stakeholders to develop and improve the final design of the community. In a recent project, I developed a charter, spoke to the people managers and then ran it past the steering committee and had a good debate in that forum. They all had their chance to input into it. Then we got a key stakeholder from that group involved. Because they were part of co-creating it, they had buy-in. They enthusiastically adopted it and communicated it to the rest of the organisation.

CONCLUSION

In this chapter, you've learned about phase 1 of building your champions community. You have finalised the structure, written a role description, talked to the people managers, built a list and engaged stakeholders to create buy-in.

You now have all the foundations in place to launch your recruitment and the community. Now it's time to start planning for the launch and hosting the first forum.

The next chapter gives you the nuts and bolts of launching the community.

Take action

- Use the information in this chapter to write your charter.

- Craft a role description for your champions that captures the requirements of the position.

- Start talking with the people managers in your organisation and begin your list of potential recruits.

- Bring in stakeholders from project governance forums such as a steering committee or project board to finalise your design – this creates buy-in at all levels and ensures the community will be robust.

6

PHASE 2 – LAUNCH YOUR RECRUITMENT PROCESS AND COMMUNITY

This chapter is about recruiting and onboarding your first cohort of champions. This is an exciting moment. You're forming a group that will become a great asset for years to come – if you build and sustain it in a thoughtful way.

If you get the launch right, you're creating strong foundations to nurture and sustain the group. Your champions community needs to be grounded in the correct organisational processes and culture. That is why doing an organisational capability diagnostic is beneficial – as we talked about in chapter 2. Once established and fully formed, the community will form a life of its own and gain its own momentum.

I've refined the launch process over the last five to 10 years of using champions communities as a key part of my change management strategy for any project. I've used this concept across technology, process and system changes. I've also transitioned champions communities to longer-term collaboration and innovation communities – strong, thriving networks that support business as usual (BAU) once the project has been implemented.

Remember our three-phase process we began in chapter five? Now we're kicking off the recruitment process and the community, and setting up a place to collaborate. In the next chapter, we'll move to phase 3 – sustaining and nurturing the community long-term.

RECRUITING YOUR CHAMPIONS

You have a list of potential candidates. You've spoken to their managers and perhaps received an indication of their interest in joining the community. Now it's time to start the recruitment process by approaching the candidates directly. You can approach candidates using an email, or meet them one-on-one.

It's important to pitch this role right to attract and recruit the best and brightest in your organisation. It is also important to make the experience itself attractive so you can retain these people for the long-term.

When I was forming my first ever champions community, I did not take a structured approach. I made ad hoc requests directly to potential candidates without first getting the backing of their manager and I also didn't write a clear role description. This put the people I asked in a difficult position of having to discuss the role with their manager, which blindsided the managers and put doubt into the minds of the employees about how well supported or scoped the role was in the first place. Luckily, I learned fast – I formalised the role and got sign-off from the managers and their blessing to approach their candidates.

Craft your approach. Outline the role and why you think they're a good fit. Clearly explain the benefits of being involved and the development opportunities it will bring.

Here's a sample email script I sent to potential candidates on one project. Ideally, this communication will come from the change lead who's managing the process during the life of the project, with the manager CCed. As discussed earlier, my preference is for the manager to discuss the champion role with the potential champion prior to this email being sent. Use the following script to give you some ideas for your approach.

Dear [name],

The COVID-19 Capability and Safety Working Group supports clinical staff in using technology to minimise COVID exposure and connect with patients and their families. Many of our medical and allied health clinicians are moving to Microsoft Teams to facilitate this.

I am seeking nominations from staff who are keen to join a team of champion users who will support the whole organisation to make the best use of this new technology.

As a champion, you will receive targeted training to increase your skills in using Microsoft Teams effectively, becoming a subject matter expert who can support your colleagues through the transition and beyond. As an early adopter, you'll benefit from learning and leadership opportunities, joining a community of practice to share, collaborate and cross-fertilise with peers across the organisation.

We'll cover topics such as:

- common telehealth and other use cases

- telehealth policy

- using Teams for inpatient telehealth, ward rounds, handover meetings and specialist consults

- agile and lean methodology

- quality assurance processes

- effective communication.

Your role as a champion will involve assisting your colleagues/team to become more familiar with the navigation and additional functions of Teams, such as sharing documents, recording content for sharing later, setting up and using planner walls, and starting up different work/project groups.

Your time investment will help us all work more effectively while maintaining physical distance, and it's a great opportunity to demonstrate and develop your leadership capabilities.

If you are interested or would like to nominate someone for this role, please get in touch with me. I am also happy to answer any questions you may have about the role.

Kind regards,

[Your name]

THE KICKOFF SESSION

Now it's time to book the kickoff session, prepare the materials and run the session with your first cohort.

Create an invitation to send to your candidates. Use the emails from the list you have been building in collaboration with their managers. Remember, you have been dealing with each of the managers one-on-one or as a group to get their buy-in, nomination and ongoing support for the initiative.

Invite the managers to the kickoff meeting with champions and the executive sponsor, which covers the terms of reference, roles and responsibilities – or add them to the regular meetings if already in flight. Add them to the collaboration technology platform that you have set up.

Develop the introductory session materials for the change champions. The content should include session objectives, an icebreaker which is an opportunity for members to introduce themselves, the role overview, the governance and performance development process, the calendar of events, an overview of change management – which is optional – and introducing the concept of change leadership in this role.

Then develop all your support collateral, including FAQs. The FAQ document covers off the most common questions and it's important content to develop at this stage. The document should be aimed at all end users, with a section on the champions role – who the champions are and how to access their support. You can collect FAQs as you talk to the managers as well as the champions during the recruitment process. You could also ask one or two of your candidates who appear to be early adopters of the champion concept to review your first draft.

It's important to send the right information and plan your agenda and materials for the inaugural session carefully. Start as you mean to continue. Build trust from the outset by being professional and aligning the role to existing HR and development processes.

Remember that when forming any new group, people are attentive, want to listen more than they talk and want to be reassured that participating in the group is not a waste of their time. It's the beginning of building the trust between you and the group, as well as between members of the group. Grab their attention early and make sure they know you're in it for the long haul – and you won't exploit their time or trust.

ONBOARD AND ASSESS THE CHAMPIONS

As you recruit each member, you need to onboard them. Onboarding champions means integrating each recruit with the charter, explaining expectations and culture, as well as giving them the tools and information needed to become a productive member of the team. Map each champion to a division or team to ensure you have a good representative organisational spread. Here are some things you must do during onboarding:

- be clear about the group requirements
- be clear about the program requirements
- run through the charter and provide copies to each member
- explain the frequency of meetings and invite members to attend
- give clear guidelines on how to successfully participate in the group and program
- explain development opportunities the community offers
- give important insights into the progress and potential pitfalls of your project
- thank members for joining and for their anticipated participation.

During onboarding you can also start assessing who the early adopters, the group in the middle i.e. the early and late majority and the laggards are. This differs in organisations based on their organisational capability and maturity. I found staff in a health care organisation I worked with were much quicker to adopt change than other industries, but it was a little more chaotic. It was also just as the COVID pandemic started and they had to get online FAST! They took to their roles quickly but then we had to follow up with some strong governance and remediation of information on the platform because it grew quickly without information guidelines in place. This was very different to a bank I worked with, where members were slower to adopt and more risk averse to using new features, which meant we slowed the rollout. It took me a lot longer to establish the kickoff session in the more traditional organisation than it was in the more innovative, but the experience was probably slightly more chaotic in the innovative organisation.

DEVELOPMENT OPPORTUNITIES ARE IMPORTANT

A lot of planning is required to launch community build and then sustain it. It's all well and good to roll out a system and think it's all done and dusted once the technology rollout has been completed. But that's when the fun starts. It's all about business adoption. Why use the system? How is it aligned to the strategy? Does it fit with new ways of working? Do we know why we are using it and how it is aligned to the organisational strategic vision? What happens if we don't use the system? Is it a software implementation, process change, organisational restructure or all three? This is why it's so important to develop and train your champions – because they can add so much value here.

Identify a schedule of development opportunities. What are some learning opportunities you could offer? Just-in-time coaching with the group and individuals? Review the project timeline regularly, track your change and fill the gaps identified in your business readiness plan. Do you need to conduct train-the-trainer sessions for the system or process to speed up delivery? Is a change management 101 session necessary? The key is to upskill the champions so they are well resourced to smooth the path to BAU. More mature communities may include champion duties as part of the HR commitments to recognise the work they do.

On one large project I was involved with, every time we rolled out software to a new team there were many of the same questions. There were also some specific questions based on the team's requirements. The project team did not have the time or resources to support all staff. Our champions supported their local teams. We supported and developed our champions. We also rewarded their efforts with vouchers, awards and funding for learning and development opportunities.

Think of some activities and opportunities you could offer your champions. Ideas include getting involved in creating implementation guidelines, team building, monitoring and auditing practice, ongoing education, role modelling and peer-to-peer mentoring and coaching.

One of the risks of becoming a change champion is that the organisation will continue to value and reward you solely for your regular job duties. If the champions role is not rewarded as part of the performance process, champions will continue to prioritise their BAU role and may not take their champions responsibilities seriously. You need to pull out some KPIs and development opportunities specifically for the champions role and build it into champions' own job description.

Doing this is a nice way to articulate champions' value to the organisation. Champions get a real kick out of helping the organisation and helping their teams, and it's good to recognise them. Often it's not a financial bonus that is important to them, it's being acknowledged for their contribution to their peers and possibly across the organisation. If you don't build their champions role into their job description, it gets lost in their everyday activities. The champions' tasks get loaded on top of their BAU role without any real recognition of what they're doing.

In a recent project, I offered the champions group some training for the whole group and negotiated with their managers to have a day out of their BAU role. The training was in agile, managing scrums, lean process design and developing processes. These were great skills for them to take back to their teams and use in their day-to-day operations.

It was also a great team-building opportunity – they enjoyed getting to know their peers within the champions community and built trust.

Start this important new engagement process with HR and people managers. Produce a draft of the KPIs, approved bonuses and list of development opportunities – both core and individual KPIs, suggested training opportunities and possible training providers. Discuss it with the champions, update the role description, and then prepare a checklist for the people manager to incorporate discussions about the champions role and responsibilities in their next performance development discussion with their team's champion.

LAUNCH A COLLABORATION PLATFORM

Now you've kicked off the community, you need an online place to collaborate, nurture, build and support the community to stay engaged. Launch a collaboration platform for the champions to chat, get to know each other and share information. Use software such as Microsoft Teams or Facebook for work. It needs to be a secure platform and preferably part of your existing IT tools. This is a place you can meet, virtually chat, share documents, brainstorm, plan initiatives and track tasks. I go into more detail on how to set up a technology platform in chapter 8.

Collaboration technology needs to be managed and regular posts made by the person managing the group. Make it a safe place to ask questions, raise issues and collaborate with peers to cross-fertilise. I've used Microsoft Teams successfully to build and interact with champions in the last five projects I've been involved with. It is a ubiquitous tool and most people know how to use it. It was closely managed and I was posting regularly – a couple of times a day at least – until the groups started trusting the platform and talking among themselves.

TELL THE BUSINESS

Now you need to market and communicate the launch of the champions community. Ensure everyone across the business is aware of the change champions community.

Ideally, this message about the importance of the network will come from the project sponsor or a senior leader. Communicate the purpose and strategy of the champions community as part of the organisation-wide launch. Announce where champions can be reached and how employees can learn from the champion within their team. Encourage interested employees to learn more about the champions community and provide them with guidance around how to get involved.

This will make the organisation aware of this important support channel – these champions or employees who understand their issues at the coalface. An awareness campaign attached to a specific project launch is a good way to communicate and spread the word. As part of the campaign, including messaging around the fact that people feel more comfortable asking their workplace colleagues questions about new processes and systems. The champions can advocate for the change, smooth the transition and ensure people adhere to consistent processes, policies and ways of working. That can also be the canary in the coal mine, or the early warning system for any persistent technical and/or usability issues.

Sometimes there's a pattern or theme in issues that arise and if you're seeing it across each of the divisions, then you know it could be a systemic problem and probably needs to be raised as a defect if it's an IT system, or you need to communicate or work out an action plan to solve it.

In large organisations, I use a social platform to promote the group. Get permission from each champion to publish their name as the go-to person within each team and division first. Spread the word and keep it going across different channels and audiences. Have an email contact address or a way of contacting the champions of change.

Draft your communication campaign for launching this group in plain English. Who are you trying to reach? What message do you want them to receive? How will you try to reach them? These are simple questions with often complex answers that a document plan can help clarify. Who benefits from having such a plan? You'll benefit from documenting an actual communication strategy rather than just winging it.

Some things to think about when you're developing a plan:

- identifying the purpose of your communication
- identifying your audience
- planning and designing your message
- considering your resources
- planning for obstacles and emergencies
- strategising how you will connect with others who can help you spread your message
- creating an action plan.

CONCLUSION

Now you've recruited and launched the first cohort of your champions community, you can start building this into a vibrant group who can become user advocates – the voices of their teams.

Once you've reviewed the tips and tricks in this chapter it's time to get cracking.

Now you have formed the group you need to do a succession plan to set up your champions for long-term success.

Take action

- Be thoughtful about how you recruit your champions community members.

- Plan your onboarding process to set your champions up for success.

- Brainstorm some development opportunities you can integrate into the program.

- Launch a collaboration platform to help members communicate.

- Tell the business about the champions group and market its benefits.

7

PHASE 3 – SUSTAIN AND NURTURE YOUR CHAMPIONS

Now you've done the hard work of identifying, educating and meeting with your champions for the first time, you need to keep building momentum by nurturing the group and building trust. The right online platform to build engagement and support can really help with this process – I'll discuss this further in chapter 8. Whatever platform you use, you will have to do some heavy lifting for at least the first couple of months – but the results will be worth it.

Building trust with this group is key. You need to schedule a timetable of activities, forum topics, training and support opportunities for the group to learn and grow as individuals and as a group long-term.

The champions need to know they're not wasting their time and effort investing in this group.

Being strategic and having an action plan is recommended. It will give you a run sheet of activities and cadence. Remember, this group is on the frontline and can give you early warning signs, so listen carefully to them.

Setting up a thriving champions community will build skills and knowledge that can be utilised even once your official project is over and you're back to BAU. For example, one community I set up continued to be a thriving community when the project finalised, and became instrumental in providing workplace support to peers. They managed a backlog of future development, prioritising it and advocating for the development of high-priority features to the BAU governance forum. It takes a lot of time and effort to set up and manage a champions community, but their support across your organisation will be priceless. Remember, you are also taking some time from the champions' BAU roles, so make sure you keep spelling out the benefits of this group to the wider organisation.

This chapter outlines some key considerations and activities that sets champions up for success and starts adding to the champions change toolkit.

DEVELOP THE CHAMPIONS' CHANGE RADARS

Now's the time to start skilling this group up in change management know-how. This skill serves anyone in a dynamic world, in both personal and professional spheres. A simple way for champions to lead and manage their teams and users is to give them a change framework to use. It's also wise to adopt the framework for your own use when inter-acting with the champions group. There are many to choose from.

LISTEN, COMMUNICATE, PARTICIPATE, ADVOCATE AND DEBRIEF

The first phase of doing this is to communicate and listen. Share information with your champi-ons about your projects and actively listen to their concerns and feedback to the project team. Then lead and prioritise – demonstrate or model behaviours you expect from your champions and prioritise key activities. For example, you might promote training.

The next phase is to participate. Where required, organise workshops to ensure the project is on target for your team or teams.

The third phase is to advocate – to positively discuss your initiative with your team of champions. If you buy in, there's a higher likelihood they will too. Recognise and acknowledge individuals in your team, demonstrate a new way of working and share successes with the project. A poor first experience influences adoption of any change. Expect resistance – people are invested in current ways of doing things.

The fourth phase is to debrief. Add a standing agenda to your regular forum for the champions to debrief, ask questions, raise issues and deal with resistance. They can also give the same opportunity to their teams, but it requires the right skills and careful management.

It's important to discuss with your champions the best ways to articulate the value of the change you're implementing. How can they help their teams to use a piece of software to get the most out of it? How can they ensure their team members know the different features and how to utilise them? If it is a change in process organisational structure, how can this change help with their team's day-to-day performance?

SUPPORT YOUR CHAMPIONS

One of the biggest things for any user adoption is lack of support. The key for anyone supporting champions is to help solve their problems. Keep checking in with them, be across the latest new features of systems and new ways of working and keep communicating. Ask the champions to cascade important messages to their teams and leaders, as they know the best channels for their local area and they have relationships and influence.

It is hard for many people to change, even when it's positive. It's important to sustain excitement and momentum to make the experience for your users a positive one. It's also important to give the champions a safe space to raise questions, concerns and good news stories about their recipients of change as well as about the community as a whole. They can celebrate their successes, share their burdens and try to solve their problems. For example, in one organisation, I made a standing agenda item for each champion to share a problem within their team, how they solved it and lessons learned. Often, there were some great innovations that came because when one champion raised an issue, a few of them would say, 'Oh, I'm having that same problem.' They'd get together and come up with some sort of solution and propose it to the development team. Often, these ideas got developed.

KEEP BUILDING MOMENTUM

You need to be strategic about building momentum – but don't overdo the level of activity you expect from your champions. Keep checking in and validating the pace and your expectations of their level of involvement and commitment.

Here are some tactics I've used in the past to engage and build momentum:

- Continuously meet with champions to learn how they're doing and gather feedback about how their teams are finding new ways of working.

- Ensure a regular rhythm for discussions with the champions around what's working and what's not.

- Design a program to engage and recognise their efforts – such as providing privileged access to relevant events or speaking engagements.

- Identify and encourage your natural leaders in the group – they naturally bubble to the top and even when they don't have positional power, they are key to your success.

- Identify the early adopters in your group and encourage them to start posting on your collaboration platform alongside you.

- Give something back – recognise the work that champions are doing through public recognition and awards.

- Kick off a 'voice of the community' blog and ask champions to do guest blogging – this will help build case studies and bring examples to life while giving the author a chance to showcase their work and their role in their team.

It's important to build this momentum for them as a team and make it a normal part of business.

On a recent project, I approached four of our champions to provide their story and experience of using a particular piece of software. I interviewed each one and drafted their case study using a standard template. After a review I published their stories on the project intranet site. Distribution was to all staff and it had a good readership. This is a great way to profile their challenge, their resolution and the project benefits.

KEEP COMMUNICATING TO THE BUSINESS

Continue communicating with individuals and the organisation about the champions role and its benefits. Remember, the champions are your business representatives to their teams. Ensure they don't become part of the IT service desk function or caught up in any other BAU support teams.

Part of the success of one community, where I built an enterprise IT system rollout, was to build a strong and thriving champions community to execute a strong business readiness plan. A business readiness plan is a set of approaches and metrics to track usage and gauge people readiness.

We defined some metrics to track success. For example, when rolling out Microsoft Teams for the first time we measured the number of emails being sent compared to the number of posts, reactions and responses and a team leader board of who was using the platform most often instead of emails. The champions proactively prepared their teams by being transparent about how their engagement was being tracked and ongoing.

BUSINESS READINESS AND ADOPTION

Keep your project team and extended change community focused on business readiness and adoption. The technical stream of a project will design, develop and deliver technology. The people stream will help users embrace, adopt and get the most out of the technology. Both streams need to be ready at go live to ensure results, outcomes and success. Both the technical and people streams of any project have a seat at the table and the ability to halt progress before going live.

If the separate areas are not focused on adoption or communicating regularly, there's a possibility that, for example, the IT stream will be ready to go live and your business adoption stream isn't. Maybe the business adoption stream has been focused on developing collateral and liaising with senior stakeholders. There hasn't been enough communication because the timing wasn't right to start or the training to end users has not been completed. For whatever reason, the users are not ready. It would be a no-go decision from the user adoption stream and one of the main sources of intelligence for this is your champions network.

I've been part of technology teams that want to run the show with no perspective on ensuring the end users of the technology are prepared and ready to go. There have been many unsuccessful rollouts where users don't feel heard or understood when using the system. They have messy workarounds, clunky interfaces and just plain stupid user design. On one project, a large collaboration technology rollout to 25,000 staff was staggered to roll out to the three divisions separately, spaced out two weeks apart. The staff in the first rollout were the most prepared and excited for the change. Once they were using the technology we started getting good feedback from them, which we could then publicise to the next two divisions. We had more time to prepare those divisions, which was the decision from the business readiness stream.

To avoid some of the common issues around user adoption it helps to do the following:

· communicate early and often

· ensure that the technology and people streams are aligned and flowing together

· build knowledge and skills of the IT Help Desk staff, allowing them to triage and escalate queries and gain knowledge of the new system they will be supporting

· build a strong and ongoing champions network that will continue after the project goes live, reporting back about business requirements, issues and readiness.

WHAT HAPPENS AFTER GOING LIVE?

Once your change project goes live (is implemented in the business), you need to maintain consistent support, encouragement and engagement with your champions.

Your champions network will be able to support and answer questions within their teams. They're important for smoothing their team's transition to the new ways of working or onto a new system. They can give you and the project team feedback on how it's going and whether further changes are needed.

Your champions are going to need the most support at the go live moment because everyone's going to be bombarding them with questions.

In a recent project, I was posting regularly on our collaboration technology in the lead-up to and the days following go live. I scheduled a meeting with the champions the day after going live. I had a special email address set up for the champions to be able to email me, so I could answer questions quickly. If champions raised a ticket to the IT service desk, then I was CCed on that particular ticket. I could follow up and manage the resolution quickly with the IT service desk, and communicate back to the champion.

The warranty period – the time in which the project team supports the business before transitioning support to BAU – is normally is about six to eight weeks. It's busy in the first week and if it's bumpy, a lot of support will be required. The champions network is an important channel to get messages out to the business but they're not the only channel, so it can be very intense.

It can help to give your champions a simple way to track the change impact (how well their teams are adopting change), such as a dashboard. Also give them easy to access calendars of events and change roadmaps, which you can track and review at every forum.

Visit the 'resources' page of my website **suewebster.co** to download a sample impact change assessment spreadsheet you can use for your organisation.

BUILD A PIPELINE

It's important to keep recruiting new champions and building a pipeline once your project has been implemented. At this stage, you have to decide on the ideal number of champions your initiative, bearing in mind that people will move on from their champions role for many reasons.

You should also assess how effective your champions are and whether you need to bolster numbers in certain areas, or replace champions who are not getting traction with others.

In one project I was involved with, I posted an overview of the champions role as part of the initial recruitment, asking for volunteers on the enterprise's Facebook page. It worked and we got 10 really great champions. I have also asked for referrals from other champions because they knew the job, what the role entailed and many had good contacts. I asked managers at steering committee meetings. I kept my eyes and ears open for people.

Have a separate tab in your candidates spreadsheet for potential new candidates and note where you're up to in the recruitment process for each person.

Utilise your collaboration platform and the wider community via your social media network, if you have one, to identify who is helping new users and has the potential to grow as a new champion.

CONCLUSION

Gaining momentum in your champions program and growing it over time is key to this group's success. It will benefit your organisation as a whole when you start thinking about long-range goals you want your champions to help you achieve.

Build your champions up as ambassadors for your project in partnership with you and your project team. Don't be tempted to let the champions community wane once the project is completed. It will have ongoing benefits.

Work through the steps I've given you to build, retain and continue the champions group in a clear and focused way.

In the next chapter, we'll go into the details of setting up the collaboration platform to build trust, share information with the group and support each other.

Take action

- Make a plan to invest in your champions' knowledge of change management.

- Invest in activities that will keep the momentum of your community going.

- Plan to provide additional targeted support leading up to and in the days after going live.

- Ensure you have a pipeline in place for when champions leave the group.

8

COLLABORATION AND SERENDIPITY

In a collaborative culture, cross-functional teams work towards a common objective. They have built the processes, systems and organisational structures to make it easy for people to work with anyone across the organisation to deliver the best product and/or service – starting with a thriving champions community.

Traditional organisations are not designed for creativity; they are designed for planning and control. They assume the way they operated in the past is the way to keep going. Their success is about executing business plans and their employees are divided into discreet, functional departments.

This chapter is about starting small, and getting and staying more agile. Use it to model new ways of working, including the collaborative culture that agile organisations need.

Innovative companies operate from different assumptions and understand that the future is probably very distant from the past. Their business success is based on adapting to the evolving markets and organising people to enable the constant cross-pollination of ideas. Innovation flows from unusual connections among people, leading to serendipity.

THE POWER OF SERENDIPITY

Serendipity is when you find the ideas you weren't looking for, but that turn out to be valuable. Traditional organisations have trouble innovating because their organisational cultures and structures do not allow serendipity. Serendipitous discoveries emerge from connections or insights you get when searching for one thing only to find something else. You discover ideas you didn't know of or didn't consider until that moment of insight.

Some issues frequently linked to a lack of collaboration include not having a cohesive organisational culture; instead, the organisation works in silos leading to interpersonal barriers to collaboration. Byproducts of this kind of working include a lack of respect and trust, fixed mindsets, poor listening skills, knowledge deficits, a lack of alignment around goals, internal competitiveness and information hoarding. Collaborative organisations bring people and the organisation closer together to cross-pollinate ideas, problem-solve, learn from each other, be more effective and open up new communication channels. This, in turn, boosts morale, employee engagement and retention – and these conditions lead to a competitive advantage.

COLLABORATION UNLOCKS CREATIVITY

Collaboration is a way of thinking. Great things can happen when we work together, and there is an undeniable strength in teaming up. Building new ways of working as a collaborative culture is the secret to unlocking the creativity hidden inside your daily work and giving every great idea a chance. Don't set up an innovation department – instead, change the fundamental DNA of your organisation to allow serendipity to happen.

Some examples

Larry Sanger, once editor of the struggling online encyclopedia Nupedia, learned about wikis from a friend over dinner and then renamed his revamped project Wikipedia. A wiki is a website or database developed collaboratively by a community of users, allowing any user to add and edit content.

Another example of serendipity is the idea of combining a phone and your library of music. It was an unusual connection that no-one had ever thought of until the iPhone. Steve Jobs understood that serendipity was the pathway to creativity and innovation. He never divided Apple into functional divisions. He created an environment where engineers and designers constantly rubbed shoulders to enable these serendipitous possibilities to emerge.

Virgin Pulse's motto is 'One Team One Dream', and the organisation practises this through constant collaboration and communication, mutual respect and adopting the mindset. Staff are all in it together. Face-to-face time, both online and offline, helps its teams collaborate. It has 11 offices globally, and finds that connecting and collaborating across these offices is critical to success. That's why it selected a collaboration toolset and trained staff to use it.

According to research published in the *American Psychologist* journal there are three fundamental elements to successful group work regardless of setting:

- **Proximity:** the team's ability to easily connect and share

- **Information permissiveness:** how easily a team shares ideas, ask questions and searches for new insights and opinions

- **Familiarity:** the sense of camaraderie.

The higher a team scores in these three, the more efficient it is. If your team struggles in these areas, it will be necessary to build a collaboration culture. The organisational culture usually reflects the dominant collaboration methods. Time building your collaboration culture is time well spent. You can create great teamwork and trust within your teams, and they can then be more innovative and more productive, both online and offline.

Organisations won't be successful if there's a lack of trust and low morale. Collaboration is key to moving forward. It helps if you encourage new ways of working to create the conditions for innovation and serendipity.

This is where technology comes in.

WHAT IS COLLABORATIVE TECHNOLOGY?

Collaborative technology refers to tools and systems to help a group work both in the office and remotely. It allows for more intuitive and coordinated group problem-solving across an entire team's workflow. It integrates both teamwork and tasks and helps the team to coordinate work tasks and activities.

Being productive outside the office means using tools that help teams be more communicative, collaborative and cooperative than ever. What seems like a straightforward series of software and hardware is a web of evolving collaborative tech products, each with its own capabilities and bene-fits. To work out what will work best in your team, you need to know how collaborative tools are classi-fied. Here are some of the most-used types of tools:

- **Document management software:** Used to create, edit, design, review and approve documents. It provides a central repository for employees to access those documents on any device.

- **Time management software:** Your digital calendar with scheduling, notifications, event alerts and even payroll capabilities.

- **Project management tools:** Workflow software to oversee a project's end-to-end execution across team members' responsibilities and activities; interactive and more dynamic than a static project plan.

- **Information-sharing software:** Notification-based applications where individuals can send updates and alerts after they've completed a task or checked off a project part, and ask direct questions or send messages to the right person.

- **Knowledge management and creation tools:** Single-project database sources with bookmark saving and tagging, data entry, querying for quick searches and information-based inputs. Lately, AI and machine learning can do automated meta-tagging. Metadata is used by browsers (to display content or reload a page), search engines (keywords), and other web services.

Some examples you may already be familiar with include your emails, instant messaging and chat forums, and sharing digital whiteboards to brainstorm and update data. You might share calendars and scheduling tools, and you may have project management software and Kanban boards.

Here's an example of how the different technologies can be used. Let's say you're an executive manager managing a group of people producing board papers. Your team has strict deadlines and different people writing different topics. To manage all the different papers and deadlines, you set up a spreadsheet in Excel – but over time, you've realised that none of your team members consistently view or update it. To get around this you have been manually checking every day and prompting the laggards by email. All the sharing and collaboration to do with the work happens via email, which is confusing – and often, information gets lost. It is difficult to track the progress of tasks as a team.

So, you have decided to implement a digital planner board with integrated apps. This will help the team manage the process and give visibility to the whole team. People will complete their tasks on the planner board and then chat online. This will make them much more productive, saving them a couple of hours per person across the month. It saves time as a planner board can be viewed and updated by any member at any time. During team meetings you can filter tasks by team members, track progress and make changes during discussions. It will also save you time, as automatic notifications mean you will no longer have to manually check and nag your staff. In fact, you'll save around five to 10 hours a month in manually tracking tasks. You'll spend more time editing content, thinking about upcoming board papers and doing more qualitative work – much more valuable tasks for a leader to be focusing on.

START WITH LEARNING

The first step before implementing any new technology is to understand your employees. You need to be across individual use cases, their pain points, how they want to collaborate and how they're going to connect. Build that into your culture and you'll have the right foundations in place for software to work. Be clear on your ways of working and what you want to achieve from implementing the new collaborative tools. Begin by looking at your change capability. Start building your community and then set up your continuous change culture.

WAYS TO ENGAGE

Offer a Myers-Briggs Type Indicator (MBTI) assessment and do a team playback to reflect on how the different MBTI types may work together. The MBTI is Jung's theory of personality types. Discuss type preferences and how the preferences pair works. It can be used to get the most out of how each of the types work individually and what they can bring to a team. This will initiate a lot of conversations.

In past collaboration technology projects I've been involved with, we used personas to work out the different needs for collaboration across the organisation. For example, in a healthcare organisation, we looked at how doctors, mental health teams, nurses, office staff and knowledge workers would collaborate. We then came up with simple examples of how each group would like to collaborate.

We talked to the Microsoft Success Manager for the industry sector, who put us in touch with some other health care organisations. We found out how they'd implemented similar technologies in their organisations. Microsoft supplied us with a library of healthcare user scenarios. We worked with key stakeholders from each major end user segment – for example, frontline medical teams in hospitals, mental health specialists, social workers – and tailored their feedback to the healthcare organisation where I worked at the time. Some good examples came out of that, where doctors were doing ward rounds via their phones during COVID-19, and mental health groups who couldn't meet face-to-face were implementing technology solutions. We set up a use case for mental health support groups to monitor who was coming into the group and make it as interactive as possible using Microsoft Teams technology. This included sharing documents and running training sessions for the groups, and illustrating simple concepts on a whiteboard when the group was in discussions.

TRY SOME COLLABORATION TECHNOLOGIES

Trying some collaboration technologies and practices is a great next step. A good example to begin with is Microsoft Teams, which has integrated apps including email, calendar, whiteboards, project planning boards and so on. Keep in mind that teams need to be equipped with the information to make sound decisions and the tools that make collaboration easy.

As I mentioned earlier in the book, focusing on new ways of working while rolling out collaboration tools is an excellent way of doing it. You can leverage the opportunity to change the culture on one project. This means upgrading your technology while incrementally introducing new ways of working and collaborating on new software.

During COVID-19 lockdowns, when companies were forced to have their entire workforce work remotely while still being productive, they sped up their technology rollouts to accommodate a quick onboarding of their total workforce to working remotely. The staff adapted, and the culture changed forever. Companies started collaborating on these new platforms, and real-life examples of collaboration have made history.

There have been many inventions, discoveries and innovations due to the combined effort and ideas of two or more people working and collaborating. James Watson, Francis Crick, Maurice Williams and Rosalind Franklin discovered the double helix DNA structure, thanks to the combined effort of four people. Watson and Crick met at the Cavendish Lab at Cambridge University in 1951, where they studied DNA structure together. Franklin and Williams obtained high-resolution photographs of DNA through X-ray crystallography at King's College in London. Watson and Crick used this data in their research. They made physical models of DNA. All of them helped contribute to this breakthrough discovery. In the early 1950s, the race to discover DNA was on. Wilkins got frustrated with Franklin, who believed that DNA was a helix structure but did not want to announce it until she had done more research. So in January 1953, he shared Franklin's results with Watson without her knowledge or consent. This helped Watson and Crick take a conceptual leap to discover that DNA was a double helix and could reproduce itself without changing its structure.

In 1962, Watson, Crick and Wilkins won the Nobel Prize for physiology/medicine. Franklin had died. The Nobel Prize can be awarded to up to three living recipients. There still speculation as to whether Franklin would have been included in the prize had she been alive.

The point is, it is not only about technology; it's about new ways of working and building trust. When companies push collaboration without explaining the business value and purpose for the tool, projects tend to fail. For companies, rolling out new collaboration tools can be tricky – both in terms of employee uptake and making sure productive interactions between staff occur.

The answer is to work on the culture and the new ways of working, as well as the technology. It's not just about giving staff a system and expecting them to know how to use it. It's giving them opportunities to use it and encouraging them to use it by developing a culture around it.

UNDERSTAND YOUR ORGANISATIONAL CAPABILITY

There are some things you need to understand before spending big on collaboration tools. You need to assess your organisation's maturity, understand what collaboration barriers there are in the organisation and then choose a project to pilot this on.

Speak with the employees who need to connect and collaborate as part of their role. Learn about their use cases, their pain points, how they want to collaborate and how they're going to communicate with each other. For example, the board papers example we looked at earlier could involve 20 people across an organisation responsible for different topics. You could use the planner board to manage the topic life cycle, the whiteboard to brainstorm ideas during meetings, the instant chat to discuss issues further and make decisions in real time with groups of people, and then have direct access to calendars and email integrated into the collaboration platform for reminders of tasks due and meetings. You could also run virtual meetings and facilitate training sessions.

Often, some of these tools, such as social network deployments, suffer from low adoption – especially by leaders who don't see the value of building community and connections using these tools.

Encourage and coach your leaders to get on board, sell the benefits to them and ask them to lead by example.

USE YOUR CHAMPIONS TO ROLL OUT YOUR SYSTEM

Rolling out or improving collaboration technology and practices starting with your champions community is a great way to start. If you use Microsoft Teams or similar software, you can develop your online engagement strategy with this group using integrated apps such as email, calendar, whiteboards, project planning boards and so on. This could be one of the first development opportunities for this group.

This will provide an online forum for your champions to:

· Share information

· Highlight success stories

· Run forum meetings

· Run a planner board

· Have whiteboard sessions

· Share feedback.

Drive awareness among champions that highlighting and sharing their success stories on the online platform is a part of their role. Ensure they understand how sharing their successes will support the entire group. Let them know how you will gather data/evidence for the success of the change and identify hot spots and manage them in partnership with this vital community.

Whatever platform you choose, ensure there is an open space for champions to connect with one another, such as a chat group. Yammer, Slack and Google are other options.

CONCLUSION

It is time to start building a collaborative way of working with your champions. It is important to assess and understand your organisational maturity, be clear on which new ways of working you want the champions to adopt, select the right technology and start collaborating. The most significant factor in a collaborative workplace is how easy it is to share knowledge with multiple stakeholders.

In the next chapter, I'll take you through the recommended governance forums to put in place when the program team is no longer there and you have transitioned to BAU.

Take action

- Start by learning about each group within your organisation – their collaboration needs and pain points.

- Research some of the different technology options available and consider which would be most appropriate based on your organisation's needs.

- Embed the new culture and way of working as well as introducing the technology.

- Use your champions as a test case to roll out your new system.

9

GOVERNANCE AND FRAMEWORKS FOR LONG-TERM SUCCESS

This chapter will help ensure your group can keep maintaining traction when the project finishes and you – the change team and project team – are no longer there to support them and the project becomes BAU. You need to put the right people, process and governance in place to ensure the group has longevity.

Set the group up for long-term success and allow them to have a voice and influence ongoing changes to the initiative. You've worked hard on forming and building this group. The champions are depending on you. If you don't set them up for success, they will feel deflated and wonder if investing their time in this role was worth their effort. You also do not want to lose the momentum that you worked so hard to build. This momentum will help develop the right future technology and ongoing, continuous improvement within the business.

In the past, I've spoken to champions after I've left an organisation who felt let down as the community withered on the vine. Their recommendations for continuing successfully were not fully adopted by the organisation. As a result, I realised that we must do more before the project closes. For that to be successful, the ongoing plan must be signed off by the executive.

In this chapter, you will learn strategies to set up the right governance and opportunities for ongoing support and traction for the champions of change. Quite often when a project is delivered, it needs more development and advocacy. Even when a change project becomes BAU, there is a role for the champions of change in improvements, new config-urations, software, new features, new functionality and getting feedback from users. There's also the possibility of re-engaging the champions for future projects.

OUTLINE A CLEAR TRANSITION TO BAU

You need to plan a clear transition to BAU. This means covering off your BAU governance support, design prioritisation and keeping a backlog of new functionality and defects – for example, for an IT system. But you could also keep a backlog of tweaks to processes and other organisational changes. It doesn't just have to be IT.

A backlog is a list of things that come up in conversation which may need to be looked at, reviewed and prioritised for change effort or development, if it's IT.

You also need to hand over the reins to the champions group. Sometimes it's wise to select a small group of leaders within the champions group to help navigate conversations with different forums. They need to be clear on how they can manage the group and maintain their momentum.

In one project, we selected four champions to form the senior champions group. We negotiated an annual bonus for performing this senior role and defined KPIs. The managers and key executive leadership were briefed too. We also briefed the entire champions group on how it worked in BAU and the role of the small senior cohort – the lead amplifiers who communicate the feedback from the champions group to the managers. The business owner of the system led this session.

Develop a transition strategy and a schedule of activities for six months to a year after the project has been delivered.

Include the governance framework, which lists the different forums in place to make ongoing financial and strategic decisions. This also includes the way the champions group is going to form and function in BAU, and who will run it and support it.

ONGOING SUPPORT

Options for ongoing support and governance include governance forums, managers' forums, channels to add defects in future development, and the voice of the user in any ongoing changes to the initiative that was delivered. These forums are important in keeping the lines of communication open to the champions on the ground and also to senior leadership.

After the project closes, the champions can continue to ask for regular feedback from their teams; meet to discuss and prioritise current requests, defects and issues; run a backlog; attend governance forums to ask for guidance on how to solve issues and get sign-off; and give their prioritised shortlist of features and functionality for the next period and reasons why they have prioritised these items.

Think about the existing governance framework in place for the project. Can you continue to reuse it? Design a set of forums that are easy to navigate, make sense and have a clear business sponsor, a sign-off run sheet and metrics that can be tracked. Manage this discussion and set up the frameworks.

IDENTIFY ONGOING DEVELOPMENT OPPORTUNITIES

It is important to plan and advocate for some ongoing development for your champions. This is their reward for taking on a leadership role on top of their BAU role.

A champions group I recently worked with at a large insurer requested and received training in facilitation and coaching skills. There were many benefits for this training such as new confidence and skills to add to their toolkit for now and the future. We also negotiated an annual bonus for the role and specific KPIs. This meant they could discuss and track the benefits of the role with their managers in their half-year performance review. They loved it, and we felt proud we could give something back to them for their time and commitment to the role.

Develop a learning and development plan for a 12-month horizon and add the reasons why it's important. Include this in your handover activities to the business sponsor, the champions and their managers.

CONCLUSION

In this chapter, you've learned that the right governance and development is key to maintaining momentum, helping the business be self-sufficient and ensure the changes stick.

Start preparing for this at least two or three months before the project closes. Brief the business sponsor to lead these conversations with the champions and their managers. Appoint the BAU employees to be part of the governance forums. Write a governance forum charter including the purpose, the governance framework, the attendees and their role and the decision sign-off process.

Take action

- Begin working on your BAU plan several months before the project closes.

- Identify ways in which your champions can continue working in their roles once the project is rolled out.

- Consider ongoing development for the champions and have this approved prior to the project closing.

FINAL THOUGHTS

When it comes to change and helping organisations, teams, leaders and individuals through it, any inclusive, collaborative and human-focused approach will work. Your champions are an important organisational asset who can assist in fostering this approach to change and help your organisation adapt and build resilience.

The future outlook includes technology, AI and robotics. These will create exponential change in the lives of each and every one of us in myriad ways. The more people support the organisation's goals, the more people act to make a significant contribution and the more work that matters gets done. By establishing meaning and motivation, the champions can drive results at a grassroots level.

Now you know the importance of champions, you need to take the time to think about how to select, involve and support them – and keep momentum to ensure their longevity. You may get to a point where you think, is it all worth it? Press on and build this asset of people.

Develop the change champions to support your organisational goals, communicate and endorse the role at every opportunity and stick with them. Sometimes champions can get lost in the busyness of a project and competing goals.

Use the methodology I've given to get your senior leaders and managers onboard, then recruit and nurture your champions community.

I want every executive who is starting a new project to deeply understand the importance of champions of change, and that with their help we will soon live in a world where most initiatives succeed, not fail. Now it is time to become a champion of champions.

Connect with me

Visit my website **suewebster.consulting** to connect with me and download free resources, templates and tips to help you through your transformation process.

You can also join my Champions of Change LinkedIn community to connect with other like-minded change agents and see how others are implementing the ideas in this book. This is your champions of change community, which will help you get inspired and collaborate with peers and influencers.

I want to take a moment to congratulate you on how far you've come with this learning. Remember, the LinkedIn group is always there to support you if you have any questions, you'd like some clarification, or even if you just want to chat and connect.

REFERENCES

Chapter 1

PwC 2017, *Sizing the prize: What's the real value of AI for your business and how can you capitalise?*, pwc.com/gx/en/issues/analytics/assets/pwc-ai-analysis-sizing-the-prize-report.pdf.

Gartner 2020, 'Gartner Predicts 69% of Routine Work Currently Done by Managers will Be Fully Automated by 2024', gartner.com/en/newsroom/press-releases/2020-01-23-gartner-predicts-69--of-routine-work-currently-done-b.

Chapter 2

Organisation Development Tools Institute 2021, 'Organisation Capability Maturity Framework', org-cmf.com/en-gb/pages/home.

Chapter 3

Gregor Jarosch, Ezra Oberfield and Esteban Rossi-Hansberg 2021, 'Learning from coworkers', *Econometrica*, vol. 89, no. 2, pp. 647–676.

Microsoft 2020, 'Build a champion program', view. officeapps.live.com/op/view.aspx?src=https://fto 365dev.blob.core.windows.net:443/media/Default/ DocResources/en-us/Adoption/Build_Champions_ Program_Guide.pptx.

Chapter 8

American Psychologist, vol. 73, no. 4, 2018.

ABOUT THE AUTHOR

OVER 20 YEARS' EXPERIENCE. A LONG LIST OF IMPRESSIVE CREDENTIALS.

Sue Webster has been at the heart of many successful change programs and has a track record of delivering. She is good at collaborating and producing results that the organisation ultimately owns. Her talent is initiating and driving highly engaged and positively minded communities that own, implement and inspire change both upwards and downwards within their organisation. Once she has helped set up and build the community, she loves enabling them to grow, develop and take ownership and run with it themselves.

She has worked with many household companies in Australia including UNSW, CBA, NAB, AMP, government agencies such as TAFE, the Department of Housing, Director of Public Prosecutions and the Australian Defence Force.

Sue is professionally accredited with the Institute of Coaching and Consulting Psychology and the Institute of Executive Coaching. She is a member of the Australian Psychological Society (APS), Career Development Association of Australia (CDAA) and Change Management Institute (CMI). She holds a Graduate Certificate in Career Development, a Masters (Research) in Cognitive Science and a Bachelor of Arts (Linguistics and Cognitive Science).